Why do we dream?

T0321493

Contents

Written by Isabel Thomas

Collins

1 What did you dream about last night?

While you sleep, your
body is less **active** than usual.
Your brain seems less active too.
You stop reacting to sights, sounds and smells
that you would normally respond to.

But many of us wake up remembering
strange adventures ...

Perhaps you flew through your school or zoomed
into space. Perhaps you chatted to a famous person
from history, before riding off on a phoenix!

Thoughts, **images** and feelings that happen in
your mind while you sleep are known as dreams.
Almost everyone dreams – but why?

People have been trying to
answer this question for
thousands of years!

2 Ancient ideas about dreams

Ever since writing was invented, people have recorded their dreams.

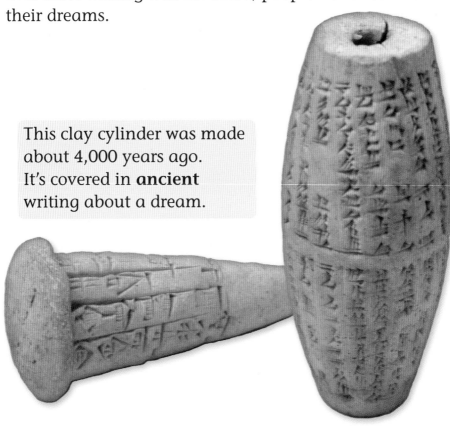

This clay cylinder was made about 4,000 years ago. It's covered in **ancient** writing about a dream.

The Ancient Egyptians believed dreams could predict the future. One prince dreamt that the Great Sphinx told him to clear up the sand around it.
The pharaoh obeyed!

The **pharaoh** built a stone pillar between the Sphinx's paws, with his dream written on it.

Ancient Egyptians visited a "Master of the Secret Things" – a cross between a doctor and a priest – to ask what their dreams meant. Dreaming about a snake was good, but dreaming about munching a cucumber was bad!

pillar

In Ancient China, people also thought dreams carried important messages. When they needed help, they visited special places to sleep and hopefully dream a helpful dream.

A famous Chinese thinker called Shen Kuo dreamt about a perfect place in the mountains. He was amazed to come across it in real life! He built a house there and called it "Dream Pool".

Ancient Chinese thinkers asked questions about dreams, too. One was called Chuang Tzu. When he woke from a dream about being a butterfly, he asked:

The Ancient Greeks wrote dream dictionaries which told people what their dreams might mean. Ancient Greek doctors even tried to use dreams to **diagnose** diseases.

If you dream that you are flying it means good luck. The higher above the ground, the richer or more powerful you will be!

The idea that dreams carried hidden messages lasted for a long time. Just 100 years ago, a doctor called Sigmund Freud became famous for saying that our dreams show what we most want, deep down.

Today, doctors and scientists have found evidence that dreams don't have secret messages and meanings. Dreams happen because our brains are busy working while we sleep!

3 The science of dreams

About 100 years ago, scientists began to study dreams by **observing** people while they were asleep.

Sleep scientists set up special **laboratories**.

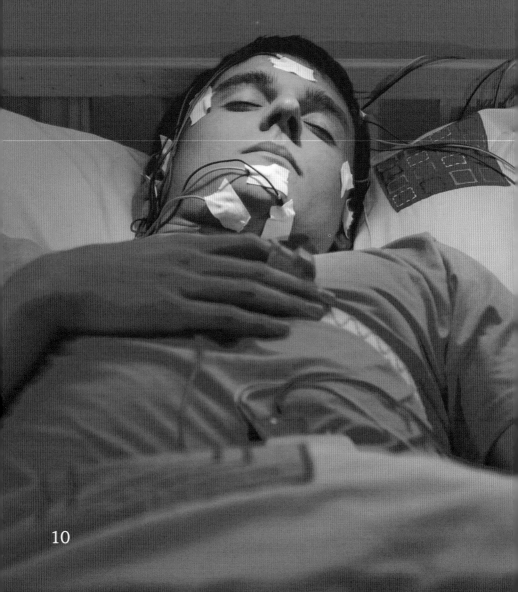

Instead of looking for differences in what people dreamt about, they looked for features of sleep that were the same for every person. They looked for patterns.

It might seem boring to watch a sleeping person. From the outside, it looks like their body and brain are switched off. But scientists soon discovered that a sleeping brain is hard at work!

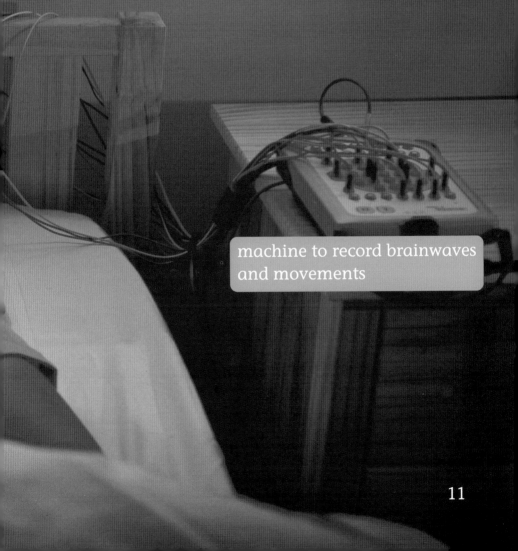

machine to record brainwaves and movements

Eugene Aserinsky was one of the first sleep scientists.

He watched babies dozing. He observed that their eyes sometimes moved quickly from side to side beneath closed eyelids. He decided to find out if the same thing happened in older children.

The first volunteer was Eugene's eight-year-old son, Armond. Eugene built a machine that could measure Armond's eye movements and brainwaves, all night long!

Every time Armond's eyes moved, the machine recorded marks on a roll of paper.

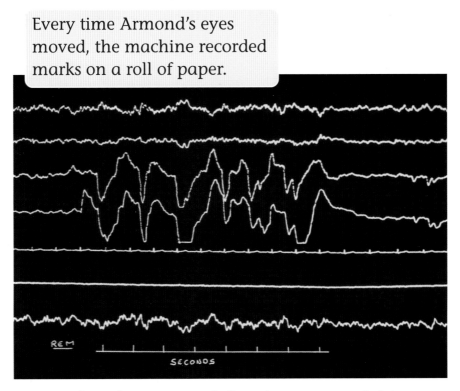

Eugene found a pattern. A few times every night, Armond's eyes darted around under his eyelids for about 20 minutes.

Eugene called this special type of sleep "**Rapid Eye Movement**" (REM) **sleep**.

After Eugene's amazing discovery, lots of other scientists began studying sleep.

They discovered that our brains aren't really resting as we sleep. Every night, our brains go through four different "stages" of sleep. This takes about two hours, then the cycle begins again!

The sleep cycle

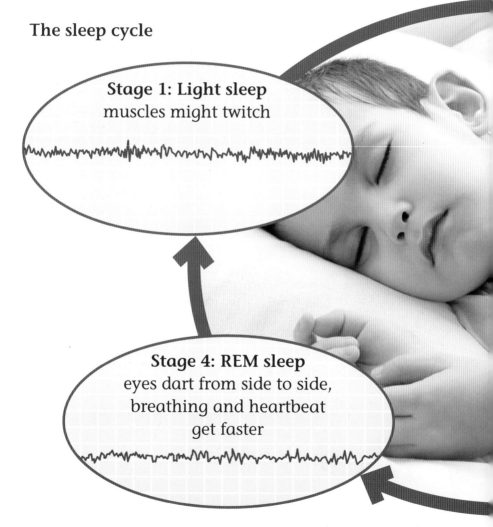

Stage 1: Light sleep
muscles might twitch

Stage 4: REM sleep
eyes dart from side to side, breathing and heartbeat get faster

Scientists noticed another pattern: most dreams seem to happen when we are in stage four – REM sleep.

So, to understand why we dream, we need to understand REM sleep better.

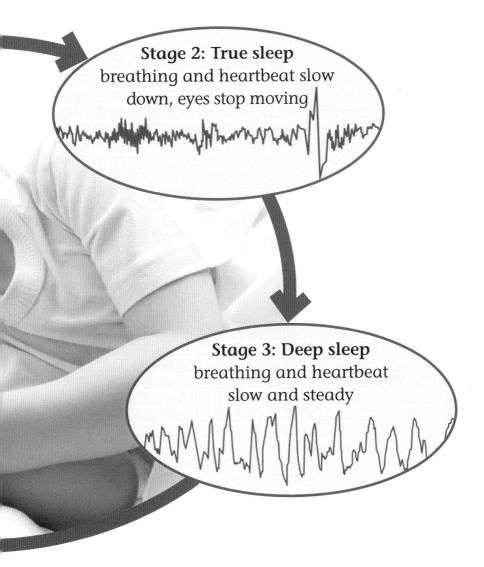

Stage 2: True sleep
breathing and heartbeat slow down, eyes stop moving

Stage 3: Deep sleep
breathing and heartbeat slow and steady

Today, scientists can use high-tech scanners to take pictures INSIDE a sleeping brain!

Our brains are made up of billions of **nerve cells** that send tiny electrical **signals**. A scanner measures these signals and works out which parts of the brain are most active.

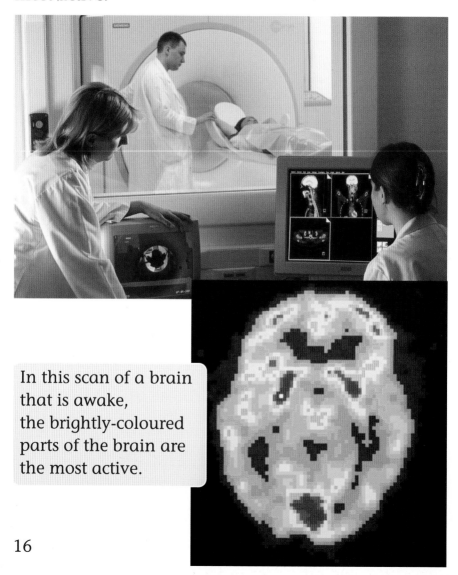

In this scan of a brain that is awake, the brightly-coloured parts of the brain are the most active.

During REM sleep, some parts of your brain are switched on, and working almost as hard as when you are awake! Other parts are switched off.

a brain during REM sleep

These parts are switched off ...

decoding messages from our eyes

thinking and making sensible decisions

using memories

making new memories

sending signals to our arms and legs

These parts are switched on ...

emotions

creating brand new images

paying attention

These patterns help scientists explain some of the strange features of dreams.

Because these parts are switched off ...

Strange things can happen in dreams that could never happen in real life.

We can't think and make good decisions. We might do things in dreams that we would never do in real life.

Dreams are hard to remember.

Our body switches off our arms and legs, so we don't act out our dreams. This keeps us safe.

Because these parts are switched on …

We can feel just as happy, sad or frightened in a dream as when we are awake.

Most people see very vivid and detailed images in dreams.

The images we see in dreams are created here! They often change quickly, so dreaming can feel like you are taking part and watching at the same time!

We know that dreams happen when parts of our brain are hard at work during REM sleep.

Other parts of our brain are switched off, which explains why dreams sometimes seem so strange compared to real life!

Most people spend up to a quarter of their sleep in REM sleep. This adds up to six years of dreaming over your lifetime!

We still have lots of questions about dreams.

- Why are certain parts of our brains so busy in the night?
- Does dreaming help us?
- Why are some dreams nice while others are scary?

To answer these questions, scientists are studying sleep and dreaming in animals.

4 Do animals dream?

Animals can't tell us if they dream. Instead, scientists must look out for clues!

Eugene Aserinsky noticed that his dog Bruno seemed to have REM sleep. A few times every night, Bruno's eyes moved quickly from side to side under his closed eyelids.

Dogs' legs often "paddle" while they are in REM sleep, as if they are acting out their dreams.

Since then, scientists have observed signs of REM sleep in many different animals, from cats to Australian bearded dragons!

We know that humans dream during REM sleep. Does this mean that animals dream too?

We'll probably never know for sure. Some scientists think animals can't dream because we need language to tell stories, even in our minds. Animals don't have language like humans do.

Learning about animal REM sleep helps us to understand human REM sleep (and dreams) better.

Imagine if studying sleeping cats was your job! Sleeping cats helped scientists discover how brains switch off signals to arm and leg muscles in REM sleep, making movement impossible!

Most animals have legs and eyes. This tells us that legs and eyes are useful and important for animals.

Lots of animals have REM sleep. This tells us that REM sleep must be useful and important, too!

When a human or animal is in REM sleep, their brain must be doing something important – but what?

Scientists have found clues by studying different animals.

They have noticed that when **mammals** are in REM sleep, they can't shiver to warm themselves up, or pant to cool themselves down. This is a clue that REM sleep is linked to the way a mammal's brain controls body temperature.

Other scientists have observed that the more skills rats learn in a day, the more time they spend in REM sleep later.

Rats that missed out on REM sleep did not learn the new skills very well. This is a clue that REM sleep helps an animal's brain to practise and remember new skills!

Human brains have many things in common with the brains of mammals, like rats.

If REM sleep helps mammals learn, it probably helps us learn, too!

5 Does dreaming help me learn?

Your brain can store more information than 1,000 computers! But it can't store everything. You can't remember your whole life and replay it like a movie.

How does your brain decide which memories to store and which to scrap?

The answer might be in REM sleep – and in our dreams!

Just like rats, humans perform a new task better after a deep sleep. And the most important part of this sleep is REM or dream sleep.

As you sleep, your brain is busy replaying, practising and remembering new skills that you have learnt.

Have you ever learnt a skill so well, you can do it without thinking about it?

Like playing an instrument ...

shooting a goal ...

or riding a bike?

Over time, our brains learn to take short cuts. This is easy to see when we learn new skills, but it happens with other areas of life, too. Our brains are especially good at noticing experiences that cause strong feelings – such as fear – and creating a short cut for the future.

For example, if you ever come face to face with a shark, you don't have to pause and think, "I wonder if this animal is friendly or not?" Instead, your brain will instantly cause a feeling – ARGH! – which makes you want to swim away!

Fear is an emotion – a feeling that makes us want to act in a certain way. Emotions are a useful short cut because they help us act quickly.

Scientists have found links between emotions and dreams.

One team of scientists invited 65 **volunteers** to sleep in a lab. As they slept, the scientists measured their brainwaves. From time to time, they woke the volunteers up and asked them about their dreams.

The scientists discovered two things.

1. The dreams most likely to be remembered were strange, involving strong emotions.

2. When people experienced strong emotions in their sleep, they had strong brainwaves in the parts of their brain involved in making memories.

This is a clue that dreaming helps our brains make new "short cuts" – linking past experiences to emotions that will be useful in the future.

In fact, if we don't get enough REM "dream sleep", we find it harder to understand emotions during the day!

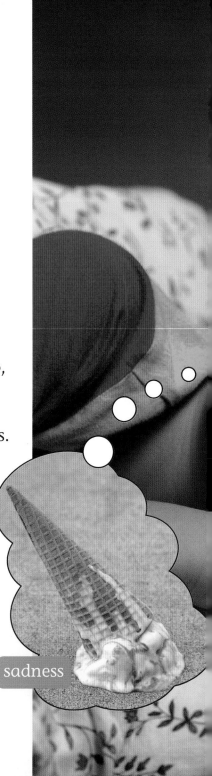

sadness

fear

happiness

33

6 What do my dreams mean?

In the past, people thought that dreams carried hidden messages.

When scientists discovered REM sleep, they wondered if dreams were just a side effect of all the jobs your brain does while you're asleep.

As scientists learn more about animal and human sleep, they think that dreams may help our brains to practise and remember new skills that we have learnt.

Dreams may even help our brains to link our memories to different emotions.

When you dream, your brain is telling stories. These stories often mix real memories with imaginary things. Often, the imagined things we dream about are linked to things happening in our real lives.

The things we dream about may not be real, but the emotions we feel in our dreams are real!

Some scientists think your dreaming brain notices which emotions you feel. Then it creates memories of these emotions in case they are helpful in the future.

This may help to keep your brain healthy. Doctors know that missing too much REM sleep is bad for **mental health**.

Britain's first astronaut Helen Sharman often dreams about returning to space!

Why do we have nightmares?

Have you ever dreamt of being lost or being chased? Frightening or unpleasant dreams are known as nightmares.

Like other dreams, scientists think nightmares might be:

- a side effect of all the work our brains do while we're asleep

or

- how our brains learn how to deal with emotions like fear, worry and sadness.

Nightmares are very common and completely normal. In fact, some scientists think they keep our brains healthy!

Most of us are lucky enough not to come across dangerous things every day. But nightmares might help remind our brain what to feel (and what to do) if we ever come across danger – like a steep cliff, or a hungry tiger – in real life!

Can we control our dreams?

People often spot links between their dreams and their real lives. But it's impossible to predict what someone will dream about.

Dreaming can feel like watching a movie. You may be the main character, but you can't control what happens!

A few people find that they can **influence** their dreams. They know that they are dreaming and can start to write the story as they go! This is known as **lucid** dreaming.

You can try to influence your dreams by thinking about certain topics as you fall asleep, or just after waking up. One team of scientists has even designed an app that helps people to shape their dreams!

7 Why do we dream?

We know that sleep is **essential** for staying healthy, but we still don't know exactly why we dream.

Scientists are hard at work testing these different ideas.

Dreams might be a side effect of our brains working hard on other tasks.

Dreams might help our brains to organise our memories and update our emotions!

Dreams might help us replay and remember new skills.

Become a sleep scientist, and you could help to solve this mystery yourself!

Glossary

active doing something, or being able to do something

ancient very old

diagnose work out what is causing an illness

essential necessary

image a picture

influence affect something

laboratories rooms specially designed for scientists to work in

lucid easy to understand; lucid dreaming is when somebody understands they are dreaming

mammals a group of animals which have fur, and feed milk to their young

mental health the health of our thoughts and feelings

nerve cell a type of cell in our bodies that can send, receive, and carry electrical messages

observing looking carefully at something

pharaoh a king or queen in Ancient Egypt

rapid very quick

REM sleep short for Rapid Eye Movement sleep; during this kind of sleep, our eyes move quickly from side to side under our closed eyelids

signals little pulses of electricity that travel along a nerve cell

volunteers people who have offered to do something

Index

The sleep cycle

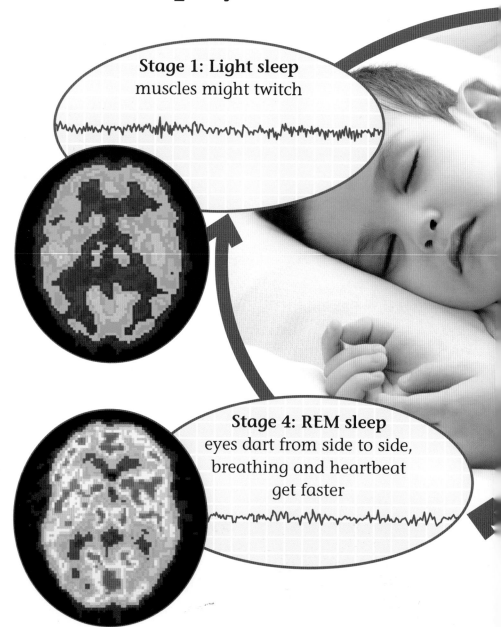

Stage 1: Light sleep
muscles might twitch

Stage 4: REM sleep
eyes dart from side to side,
breathing and heartbeat
get faster

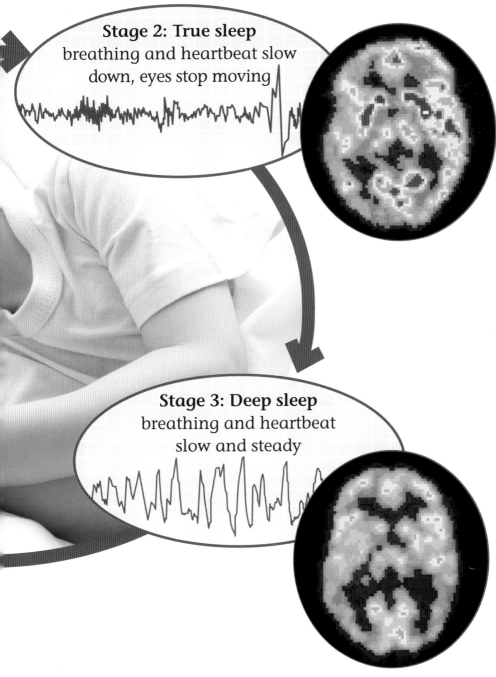

Ideas for reading

Written by Christine Whitney
Primary Literacy Consultant

Reading objectives:
- be introduced to non-fiction books that are structured in different ways
- listen to, discuss and express views about non-fiction
- retrieve and record information from non-fiction
- discuss and clarify the meanings of words

Spoken language objectives:
- participate in discussion
- speculate, hypothesise, imagine and explore ideas through talk
- ask relevant questions

Curriculum links: Science: Animals, including humans; Writing: Write for different purposes

Word count: 2585

Interest words: observing, essential, mammals, influence, diagnose

Resources: Paper and pencils

Build a context for reading

- Ask the group if anyone has ever had a dream. Ask for a volunteer to share their dream.

- Before the children see the book, read the title to them *Why do we dream?* Ask children to make predictions about the content of the book.

- Now show the cover and read the blurb on the back cover. Challenge children to ask their own question about dreams to which they hope to find the answer as they read the book.

- Introduce the words *observing, essential, mammals, influence, diagnose.* Ask children to work in pairs to suggest sentences which use two of these words correctly. Check understanding of correct usage and remind children to use the glossary when reading.

Understand and apply reading strategies

- Turn to the contents page and read through the different sections in the book. Ask for volunteers to say which section they are most interested in reading and why.